EST. PS 2020

PILGRIM SOUL
WELCOME TO THE CREATIVE CLASS

Creative Thinking Journal

IF FOUND, PLEASE CONTACT

NAME: _____

PHONE: _____

EMAIL: _____

ADDRESS: _____

_____

PILGRIM SOUL
WELCOME TO THE CREATIVE CLASS

Creative Thinking Journal

COVER ART

"Rorschach Series Abstract 0089"
by Clarence James, @pvmt84

Inspired by black culture, street-art, skate culture,
punk, underground youth culture, soul, R&B, and hip hop
music, my artwork is an exploration of truth and self.
I make abstract artwork that communicates with the
subconscious and establishes a connection between
individuals and universal consciousness.

– CLARENCE JAMES,
Washington DC street Artists and Painter

BUSINESS STUFF

ISBN: 978-0-578-87121-9

Pilgrim Soul books are available at a special discount
when purchased for fundraising, educational use or in bulk.
Special edition or book excerpts can also be created to
specification. For details, contact **INFO@PILGRIMSOUL.COM**

Printed in China
Second Printing Edition 2021

Pilgrim Soul
8033 Sunset Blvd Suite 454
Los Angeles Ca 90046

WWW.PILGRIMSOUL.COM

Creative Thinking is a competitive edge
in so many aspects of life and work.
It is about reinventing, experimenting,
growing, taking risks, breaking rules,
making mistakes and having fun.

– SHAWN GOLD,
Founder, Pilgrim Soul

How many loved your moments of glad grace,
And loved your beauty with love false or true;
But one man loved the **PILGRIM SOUL** in you,
And loved the sorrows of your changing face.

- **WILLIAM BUTLER YEATS,**
Nobel prize winning poet

Your **PILGRIM SOUL** is the native, creative explorer that is born inside of everyone.

As children, creativity is the default setting. We use our senses and instinct to discover, learn, and express ourselves without the hindrance of risk, judgment, or intellectual analysis.

The purpose of this guided journal is to help you find that kid again, and to reconnect with the inquisitiveness and wonder found in childhood that differentiates us, which we often lose sight of.

Think of this as your creative exercise book. A place for you to reframe your thinking through creative challenges, thought experiments and adult coloring pages. You will heighten creative awareness, spark imagination, bring focus to creative thinking and reflect on what makes you **UNIQUELY CREATIVE**.

HOW TO USE THIS JOURNAL

CREATIVE THINKING REQUIRES YOU TO CHANGE HOW YOU THINK. MORE THAN THAT, CREATIVITY REQUIRES YOU TO CHANGE HOW YOU THINK ABOUT THINKING.

This journal is filled with creative challenges meant to spark valuable insights so often attributed to creativity, by prompting you to think in new and unique ways.

Each challenge pushes you to rethink how you see yourself and the world around you in order to uncover new possibilities and ideas.

The challenges can be done alone or with a friend. You can do them in order or open the book to a random page and start there...it is up to you. Simply follow the instructions to complete an exercise...without self-editing or second-guessing.

If you want to share your results with fellow creative journalers, There are fun hashtags at the end of each exercise. No pressure, though, **THINK OF EACH EXERCISE AS A GIFT TO YOURSELF**.

THE CREATIVE PROCESS

In the 1926 book, The Art of Thought, author Graham Wallas points to four stages of the creative process summarized here for you:

PREPARATION

Think and study on the subject from all directions.

QUALITIES:
Open-mindedness, wonder, curiosity, and a love for learning.

MANTRA:
Learn, Discover, Explore.

INCUBATION

The germination period. Step away and daydream, walk, or meditate.

QUALITIES:
Openness, patience, flexibility and unconventionality.

MANTRA:
Listen. Gaze. Let go.

ILLUMINATION

The flash of insight, revelation,
a leap of association,
or successive leaps.

QUALITIES:
Intuition, inspirational, spirituality,
embracing the Muse.

MANTRA:
Trust your instincts.

VERIFICATION

Test the idea and determine
its validity.

QUALITIES:
Truthseeker, verifier, translator.

MANTRA:
Commit. Confirm. Refine.

THE CREATIVE MINDSET

WE'VE DERIVED THESE GUIDING PRINCIPLES AS THE FOUNDATION TO UNLOCK YOUR CREATIVE POTENTIAL.

LIMIT JUDGEMENT. When using this journal, it is essential to focus on output and let ideas flow without judgment. Just see what happens and push yourself to challenge your imagination.

TAKE MORE RISKS. Creative thinking requires a willingness to fail and make mistakes. Very often the mistake is the creativity.

CHALLENGE DEFAULT THINKING. We become so accustomed to doing things in a certain way that we lose the ability to break away and think differently. Creative ideas exist in a balance between the familiar and the new.

MINIMIZE NEGATIVE THINKING. From an early age, you've learned to analyze and criticize anything new. As an adult, it becomes second nature. Don't let this hold you back.

GO WITH YOUR GUT. If you feel whimsical, then be whimsical; if irreverent, then be irreverent...but don't pressure yourself to get it right or perfect the creative experiment.

SOME GROUND RULES...

DON'T BE AFRAID TO

Make mistakes
Laugh at yourself
Stretch yourself
Enjoy the process

STAY

Open
Positive
Encouraged
Focused

AVOID

Perfection
Judgment
Self-doubt
Default thinking

IF YOU GET STUCK

Daydream
Procrastinate
Experience life and
come back.

LEFT BRAIN

Analysis

Language

Logic

Math

Reading

Reasoning

Sequence

Speaking

Timeless

Writing

RIGHT BRAIN

Art & Music

Context

Creativity

Dreams

Emotion

Feelings

Imagination

Intuition

Personality

Rhythm

Creativity is not just for artists.
It's for business people looking
for a new way to close a sale; it's for
engineers trying to solve a problem;
it's for parents who want their children
to see the world in more than one way.

– TWYLA THARP,
Dancer, Choreographer, and Author

Creative Challenges

CREATIVE LYING

EXERCISE: In this exercise, let's test your ability to stretch the truth. Three lies and a truth. Come up with three interesting "facts" that sound real, but are not, and then one that is real. It will be a total of 4 lines. Once you've finished see if others can guess which are real or made up.

WHY?: Good fiction is the lies that tell the truth Professors from Harvard and USC business schools have found a clear link between one's ability to lie and one's ability to think creatively. In their studies, people who over-reported their success on various tasks tended to perform better in exercises that measure creativity. In short, bending the truth inherently demands creativity.

WHICH OF THESE IS TRUE?

1. One out of every ten people born in Europe this year were conceived in an IKEA bed.

2. The average person swallows six spiders a year in their sleep.

3. Coconuts are considered mammals because they have hair and produce milk.

4. In the early 1800's 99 cent stores were exclusively for the rich.

@pilgrim_soul_creative

LIST 3 CONVINCINGLY FALSE FACTS AND 1 TRUTH

1.
2.
3.
4.

1.
2.
3.
4.

1.
2.
3.
4.

Please share your #CreativeLyingPS

NAME BRANDS

EXERCISE: Anthropologists recognize naming as one of the chief methods for imposing order on perception. Just from their name, write a short paragraph describing each of these 3 people - where they're from, attire, social style, job, interests, and feel free to draw a picture.

WHY?: Screenwriting teachers will tell you that the first major decision you make about a character - their name- defines them from the get go. Somehow we become our names and our names become us. Developing a believable fictional character has our brain integrating memories and learned patterns with creative choice, which is at the heart of creative imagination.

EXAMPLE:

CONSTANCE BLEDSOE
Pointy cat eye glasses, long hair tied into braids, wears pants too high up on waist, carries a bright pink leather handbag, watches only British sitcoms, reads books and magazines three inches away from her face.

DESCRIBE THESE PEOPLE

ETHEL MCMURTRY

DONALD LENTSCH

TIFFANY BRIGGS

AUGUST GOLD

HORRIBLE POEM

EXERCISE: Write a 5-line poem that is purposefully "terrible", with whatever format or style you choose. Try just to make it the very opposite of what you or others might think is good.

WHY?: Judgment is the number one killer of creativity. On the other hand, freeing yourself from judgment is rocket fuel for the imagination. It is a healthy act of creative imagination to abandon any self-censorship completely and to just create impulsively, even going so far as creating something purposefully "bad." And, you might find that something good comes out of it.

EXAMPLE:

Better stand back
Here's an age attack,
But the second in line
Is dealing with it fine.

- Poet Laureate Andrew Motion for Prince William's 21st birthday

...Teacher, teacher, I don't understand,
You tell me it's like the back of my hand.
Should I play guitar and join the band?
Or head to the beach and walk in the sand?

- Actor Charlie Sheen

A HORRIBLE POEM

STORY SCULPTING

EXERCISE: Read through this passage from Lord of The Flies, making note of words you like or that resonate with you. Then go back and cross out what you feel are unnecessary words until you leave behind just a sentence or two that has some real, profound meaning to you. Try this with other passages in literature and share it with us.

WHY?: It's good for your creative muscles to practice chipping away, like a sculptor, to find a distinctly new idea. Often, you will find that you can best convey ideas through a simple, pared down version. Cut out the excess and make sure the heart of the matter shines through. Creative imagination often starts with uninhibited ideation, but then invariably requires editing.

His voice rose under the black smoke before the burning wreckage of the island; and infected by that emotion, the other little boys began to shake and sob too. ~~And in the middle of them, with filthy body, matted hair, and unwiped nose, Ralph wept for the end of innocence, the darkness of~~ mans heart, and the fall through the air of the true, wise friend called Piggy.

Towards midnight the rain ceased ~~and the clouds drifted away,~~ so that the sky was scattered once more with the incredible lamps of stars. Then the breeze died too and there was no noise save the drip and tickle of water that ran out of clefts and spilled down, ~~leaf by leaf, to the brown earth of the island.~~ The air was cool, moist, and clear; and presently even ~~the sound of the water was still. The beast lay huddled on the pale beach and the stains spread;~~ inch by inch.

Somewhere over the darkened curve of the world the sun and moon were pulling; and the film of water on the earth planet was held, ~~bulging slightly on one side while the solid core turned. The great wave of the tide moved further along the island and the water lifted.~~ Softly, surrounded by a fringe of inquisitive bright creatures, itself a silver shape beneath the steadfast constellations, Simon's dead body moved out towards the open sea.

- William Golding, Lord of the Flies

@pilgrim_soul_creative

STORY SCULPTING

His voice rose under the black smoke before the burning wreckage of the island; and infected by that emotion, the other little boys began to shake and sob too. And in the middle of them, with filthy body, matted hair, and unwiped nose, Ralph wept for the end of innocence, the darkness of mans heart, and the fall through the air of the true, wise friend called Piggy.

Towards midnight the rain ceased and the clouds drifted away, so that the sky was scattered once more with the incredible lamps of stars. Then the breeze died too and there was no noise save the drip and tickle of water that ran out of clefts and spilled down, leaf by leaf, to the brown earth of the island. The air was cool, moist, and clear; and presently even the sound of the water was still. The beast lay huddled on the pale beach and the stains spread, inch by inch.

Somewhere over the darkened curve of the world the sun and moon were pulling; and the film of water on the earth planet was held, bulging slightly on one side while the solid core turned. The great wave of the tide moved further along the island and the water lifted. Softly, surrounded by a fringe of inquisitive bright creatures, itself a silver shape beneath the steadfast constellations, Simon's dead body moved out towards the open sea.

– William Golding, Lord of the Flies

Please share your #StorySculptingPS   25

SQUIGGLE BIRDS

EXERCISE: A simple an effective creative warm-up from the book Gamestorming. Draw a few totally random squiggles on a page and then go back and add beaks, an eye, feet and a tail to create birds from these random squiggles.

WHY?: According to Srini Pillay, MD, of Harvard Medical School, doodling actually improves attention and memory, keeps you awake, focused and refreshed, and encourages a deep, hidden connection to the unconscious. This exercise activates and uses the pattern recognition capabilities of your brain - it's a brain warm up. And, hopefully you'll see, you don't need to be a great artist to portray an idea or imagined concept - all you need is a few squiggles.

EXAMPLE:

SQUIGGLE BIRDS

NEW WORDS

EXERCISE: These words have no meaning without you, literally. Take these made-up words and give them definitions. For extra points, write a sentence using your newly defined word in context. Who knows? It could be a thing.

WHY?: "Creating languages opened up worlds of imagination, and allowed me to create my own world," wrote J.R.R. Tolkien in his essay Secret Vice. There's a good chance you and your friends have done this to some extent already. We're continually exploring and confronting the flexibility of language. Building language, whether casual or formal, activates a primal part of the brain for expression and creativity and it's a classic builder of creative imagination.

EXAMPLE:

DEFENESTRATE
Definition: Throwing a person or thing out of a window.
Use it: 'Howard made me so cross, I had to fight the urge to defenestrate him.'

NIBLING
Definition: The gender-neutral term for nieces or nephews
Use it: 'How many niblings do you have?'

GRIFFONAGE
Definition: Careless or illegible handwriting.
Use it: 'I can never read Rupert's griffonage.'

@pilgrim_soul_creative

NEW WORDS

DREARIEN
Definition:

Use it:

CAASMONS
Definition:

Use it:

TIANLOC
Definition:

Use it:

XYRBIRD
Definition:

Use it:

PULSEMORSE
Definition:

Use it:

NEW WORDS

CROIDPEACH

Definition:

Use it:

COPESYID

Definition:

Use it:

VOLVID

Definition:

Use it:

LODGEOY

Definition:

Use it:

GREENDAMNED

Definition:

Use it:

Please share your #NewWordsPS

ABSURD SIGNS

EXERCISE: Look at the seemingly absurd signs on the next page and write the meaning for each. These signs don't have a standard, known purpose, but they do have the potential to express persuasive, meaningful warnings, or instructions. Even if it's preposterous, use defensible logic to your explanation of the sign's meaning.

WHY?: The act of thinking through absurdity activates the creative right brain. Though farce and absurdity are a relatively new tool in the timeline of creative humankind, they've made a powerful, indelible mark on the arts in the last couple of centuries. From Steve Martin to Andy Warhol, Absurdism taps into a primal, childlike openness, where rule-breaking and free association yield delightful and provocative results from a creative imagination.

EXAMPLE:

MEANING:

WARNING ROCKS ROLL UPHILL

@pilgrim_soul_creative

ABSURD SIGNS

MEANING:

MEANING:

MEANING:

FUNNY STORY

EXERCISE: Supposedly, according to science and stuff, these are the 10 most hilarious words in the English language. Create a 3-5 sentence story using the scientifically determined funniest words in the english language. It stands to reason that writing a story with so many funny words should be, well, funny.

UPCHUCK   **BUBBY**   **BOFF**

COOCH   **GUFFAW**

WRIGGLY   **YAPS**   **GIGGLE**

PUFFBALL   **JIGGLY**

WHY?: Psychologists at the University of Alberta identified the funniest words in the English language based on an average score of how it is spelled, how it sounds, how it relates to our emotions, and the meaning behind it. Their research furthers that humor, a lightened mood, and mental spaciousness are an essential additive when it comes to freeing up the mind for creativity, ideation, and problem-solving. Using these words in a story will help indulge your creative imagination.

@pilgrim_soul_creative

A FUNNY STORY

3-LINE DRAWING

EXERCISE: Start with these 3 lines and add more lines to create something recognizable. Let your mind be open to where the pre-existing lines take you, allowing your subconscious to suggest a definite object.

WHY?: Drawing is intuitive. As children, we transfer images in our head into a set of pencil strokes, even if it doesn't resemble anything. Automatic drawing, where you are given a set of lines is a way of discovering the truth of the subconscious. By starting with lines, it helps free the psyche of guilt about what you make and that produces the most intuitive pieces. It gives you more freedom from self-censorship than you would have if you sat down to purposely write or draw using your rational consciousness.

EXAMPLE:

3-LINE DRAWING

3-LINE DRAWING

Please share your #3LineDrawingPS

3-LINE DRAWING

CLOSE ENCOUNTERS

EXERCISE: Last night you traveled to a distant planet. And on that planet you saw a creature. None of its features resembled anything human-like. It was truly an out-of-this-world experience. Describe and draw a picture of your new otherworldly friend.

WHY?: Even when we are free to use our imagination, we tap into a phenomenon called structured imagination. In short, our imaginary world becomes based on existing concepts, categories, and stereotypes that we already have. When asked to think up a creature on another planet, most people draw pictures resembling life as we know it - something with eyes, ears, noses, and limbs - with the same symmetry as humans. But life forms on other planets could differ wildly and fundamentally from that found on Earth. Coming up with such a creature, without resembling a human, is a true act of creative imagination.

NEWLY DISCOVERED
Space Creature

Name:

Description:

Habits:

WHO ARE THESE PEOPLE?

EXERCISE: Go to a public place - a Coffee Shop, Supermarket, Airport - pick out two people and write their backstory. Who are they? What are their names? Are they coworkers, lovers, siblings, enemies? Why are they here? Where are they going next? If out with friends, select a few people, craft your stories, and compare results. What do you ignore that your friend emphasizes? Which details do you focus on that they might not even see? Sketch an image of two people, stick figures OK.

WHY?: People often interpret the same clues differently based on their own life experiences. This exercise can help you challenge assumptions, bypass stereotypes, and broaden the stories you create in your interactions with family, friends, and coworkers. If nothing else, it can make waiting for your coffee a bit more entertaining.

WHO ARE THESE PEOPLE?

Place:

People:

The most exciting phrase to hear
in science, the one that heralds new
discoveries, is not 'Eureka!'
but 'That's funny!'.

— ISAAC ASIMOV,
Author and Professor of Biochemistry

SLOGANS FOR THINGS

EXERCISE: A good pitchman can sell anything with a line or two. And that's your job here. Write the concise, catchy marketing slogan for these things, as if these objects might wear the sign on them for all passersby to read. Boil it down if you can to three to five words that will make us feel an appreciation or attachment to the object.

WHY?: Marketing slogans are a great example of ultra concise, lyrical, and persuasive writing. It's a challenging but highly effective form of communication to engage your creative imagination.

EXAMPLE:

FISH
"We're Smooth & Tasteful"

TREES
"The Other Valuable Green Stuff"

SPIDERS
"Eight Legs of Awesome"

PEBBLES
"Like Rocks, Only Cuter"

CLOUDS
"Think of Us as Necessary Overhead"

@pilgrim_soul_creative

SLOGANS FOR THINGS

MACHETE

LETTUCE

LUGGAGE TAGS

PURPLE CARROTS

UNICYCLES

DRY ICE

TOAST

KAZOOS

DRINK UMBRELLAS

Please share your #SlogansForThingsPS

NEW PRESCRIPTIONS

EXERCISE: Create a new prescription drug. Include the name, the problem it solves, side effects and what your healthcare provider should know before you start using it. Feel free to create a satirical drug or even a satirical version of an existing drug.

WHY?: Have you ever thought about the names of prescription drugs and how difficult it must be for those companies to keep thinking of catchy, useful sounding, appropriate names or words for new medicines? Using your own creative imagination to name something legitimizes it, makes it real and makes it a thing you can communicate more easily.

R
X **NAME:** Co-Lissen

USAGE
Co-Lissen is a prescription medicine used to enable patients to look up from their phones or devices and interact with the world.

SIDE EFFECTS
Co-Lissen may cause serious side effects, including extreme focus, sensitivity to your actual surroundings and overwhelming feelings of connections to other human beings.

Dr. Soul
Signature

@pilgrim_soul_creative

NEW PRESCRIPTION

R
 X

NAME:

_____

_____ mg

USAGE

_____ is a prescription medicine used to...

WARNINGS

Tell your healthcare provider right away if you...

SIDE EFFECTS

_____ may cause serious side effects, including...

PRECAUTIONS

Before using _____ tell your healthcare provider if you have any of the following conditions..

_____
Signature

BRUH

Please share your #AdultColoringPS

THE CREATIVE PROCESS

1. This is awesome

2. This is tricky

3. This is shit

4. I am shit

5. This might be ok

6. This is awesome

A TANKA POEM

EXERCISE: Create a Japanese Tanka poem about something in your life. Tankas are short Japanese poems consisting of five lines that give a complete picture of an event or mood. They create mental images from real-life elements, matching your emotions while writing. They can be about time, love, sadness, or any subject you need to write about.

WHY?: All poetry is an exercise in using language unexpectedly and efficiently, evoking a distinct feeling in the reader. Academic Mina Ishikawa reflects that Tanka poems often address social issues while using metaphor and the first-person, "I" perspective, elements that help foster profound personal expression, and which test one's creative imagination.

EXAMPLE:

Line 1 (3 to 5 syllables): **I POSTED A TWEET**

Line 2 (3 to 7 syllables): **AND COMMENTED ON THAT TWEET**

Line 3 (3 to 5 syllables): **MANY TIMES OVER**

Line 4 (3 to 7 Syllables): **THUS MY TWEET HAS SUCH BECOME**

Line 5 (3 to 7 Syllables): **POPULAR TO ME**

TANKA POEMS

YES TO EVERYTHING

EXERCISE: Imagine if you said Yes! To everything asked of you in a given week. This would include solicitation phone calls and emails, people asking you for stuff on the street, friends, and relatives inviting you or asking you for anything. Share 10 weekly solicitations for which you never say Yes!

WHY?: Writer Danny Wallace was told by a stranger on the bus, "Say yes more!" which led to a fantastic year in which the author said yes to EVERYTHING that crossed his path. He wrote a nonfiction book about it, which was adapted into a fictionalized Jim Carrey movie about this amazingly transformative episode in his life. But even imagining saying Yes! to specific offers that come up in your life is a mind and soul-expanding exercise, fostering your creative imagination.

EXAMPLE:

"Go to a real estate seminar, enlarge my genitalia, give my bank account # to an imprisoned African prince, buy a homeless man a fifth of gin..

@pilgrim_soul_creative

TO DO LIST

1.

2.

3.

4.

5.

6.

7.

8.

9.

10.

What made Leonardo da Vinci a genius
and different from other great minds
was creativity - a combination of
imagination and intellect.

- WALTER ISAACSON,
Historian, Journalist, and Author

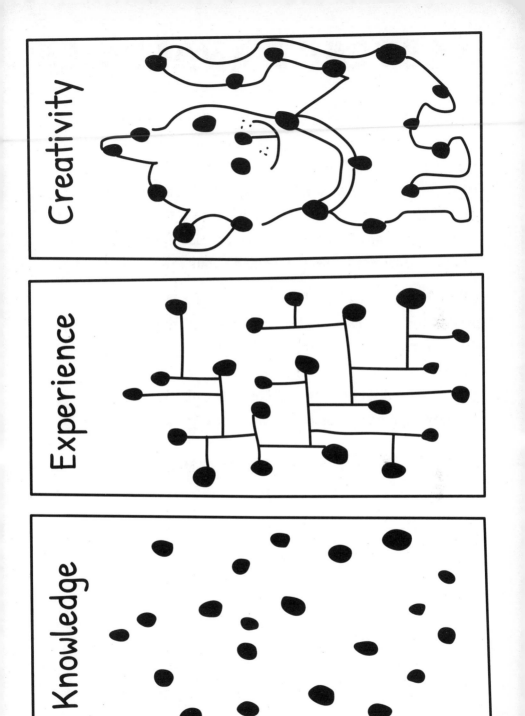

ABSTRACT ANALOGIES

EXERCISE: Take a look at the following variations of analogies for "Being in a relationship" and write out what they mean to you. Think about the nuances of these varied situations and how they trigger aspects of relationship dynamics, from your experience. By taking that problem and adding some random analogies, you can see the problem from new perspectives, thereby enhancing your creative focus.

WHY?: Analogies have been used by writers and visual artists for centuries to stimulate creative thinking by helping you gain fresh insights through discovering unexpected similarities. Choosing a random word or idea lets you approach a creative challenge from a different angle. Wishful thinking, exaggeration and escaping assumptions are ways of getting your brain past perceived limitations. You can use this innovative technique when you have a problem to solve.

BEING IN A RELATIONSHIP IS LIKE....

Cleaning the bathroom
How So? _____

Playing poker
How So? _____

Going on holiday
How So? _____

Going to the beach
How So? _____

Driving a car
How So? _____

Cooking a meal
How So? _____

Going to the gym
How So? _____

Shopping for groceries
How So? _____

Making coffee
How So? _____

Doing the dishes
How So? _____

Writing a book
How So? _____

Please share your #RelationshipAnalogiesPS   63

LOSING SPEECH

EXERCISE: You're the coach of your kid's Pee Wee basketball team and they are up by 10 points at halftime, but....you bet heavily against them. List some talking points for a halftime speech. They need to lose with dignity, while you trash your own. Convince them that losing nobly is actually winning.

WHY?: In this instance, you must balance logic and empathy with your own inner purpose to manipulate others through storytelling. Consider and understand the moral lessons that will play well with your audience (and their parents), and help you grab the cash. Threading the needle of logic here in order to get what you want is a veritable masterclass in creative focus.

EXAMPLE:

"Save your energy, don't use it all up too fast!
Slow down and make the other team think you're worse
than you are. Go for those risky 3 point shots.
Go for 5 point shots!"

@pilgrim_soul_creative

LOSING SPEECH

Please share your #LosingSpeechPS

NEW DISHES

EXERCISE: You're a MasterChef exploding on the world culinary scene. Name the main ingredients and describe the look and taste of your inventive food dishes. Feel free to be whimsical and ridiculous. What's in them? How do they look? How do they taste? How are they prepared? What was your inspiration or original influence? Tell us about the visual presentation and your unique dishware.

WHY?: Every creative task requires a willingness to open one's mind up to the unexpected. But naming is a very particular craft. Creating your story in its shortest form can be quite a challenge—especially when the goal is to differentiate your brand from the competition while staying true to the values it holds dear. It requires a creative focus that involves a combination of logic and your free-associative inner voice.

EXAMPLE:

UNDERSEA SNAKE PILLOW
A Chinese spicy sausage on a pork and cabbage ravioli covered with edible seaweed.

@pilgrim_soul_creative

NEW DISHES

ROMAN PRISONER

ANGRY FIRE ANT

DECIDUOUS CHICKEN

THAI ME UP

SEXY BANANA

Please share your #NewDishesPS

CREATIVE EXCUSES

EXERCISE: Rules are meant to be broken, especially when it comes to creativity. Come up with three believable, airtight and unusual excuses for each given situation.

WHY?: Sometimes creative performance and dishonest behavior run a parallel track. That's not to say that creative people are immoral when they take this approach, it's more that sometimes being creative involves explorations out of what we deem acceptable "truths." This exercise simulates a task that people confront in real life - fabricating excuses - not because they're malicious or greedy, but because they're avoiding punishment or shame. You can harness the creative abilities needed to do this well for artistic purposes, and the process builds focused creativity.

EXAMPLE:

An excuse when forgetting your wife's birthday.
1. How do expect me to remember your birthday when you never look any older?

CREATIVE EXCUSES FOR...

Losing someone's dog while walking it

1.

2.

3.

Getting pulled over while driving 105 miles an hour on the freeway.

1.

2.

3.

Why didn't you tell me I had food in my teeth?

1.

2.

3.

Please share your #CreativeExcusesPS

NOT IN THE FUTURE

EXERCISE: Name a few things that you think WON'T be the next big fad or trend, and why? It could be something that's never happened or something that happened already but won't happen again because it was awful or overdone.

WHY?: Thinking about the past and predicting the future requires the creative brain to balance logic and imagination, making for a rigorous task using creative focus. Trendsetting, and spotting, requires careful observation not just about what is essential right now, but what will be in the future. It forces you to relate to, and analyze, human psychology, often bringing humor and irony into the mix. Will something that feels relative now still evoke the same connection in 20 years?

EXAMPLE:

NOT BEING A DJ

Being a DJ will not be a fad in the future because everybody will already be one. Computers will make it so easy to pick the right song for the right moment that it actually becomes cool to not be a DJ.

THIS WON'T HAPPEN
in the Future

1.

2.

3.

4.

5.

FAMOUS ON TINDER

EXERCISE: Let's hook these famous characters up! Write the dating website profile "Headline" and "About Me" blurb for a well-known character from pop culture or fiction. Start with the examples then fill in your own.

WHY?: Distilling the important "bullet points" of an imaginary thing or person is a pragmatic, creative exercise geared towards finding the essential information about a person. We often use words that detract from the essence of something. Dating site profiles are a common challenge in brevity, accuracy, and persuasion, amounting to a perfect exercise in creative focus.

EXAMPLE:

NAME: Thor

HEADLINE: "Long Haired Super Athletic Surfer Type,"

ABOUT ME: I've been told I'm out-of-this-world, an intelligent but unpretentious hunk, and Nordic-meets-intergalactic. I'm as comfortable conversing over a pint of grog as flying around and fighting monsters. I have a rather unique fashion sense, a traditional way of speaking, and I'm really down-to-Earth for a (literal) god. My favorite hobby is my hammer.

FAMOUS ON TINDER

NAME: Oprah

HEADLINE:

ABOUT ME:

NAME: Donald Trump

HEADLINE:

ABOUT ME:

NAME: Taylor Swift

HEADLINE:

ABOUT ME:

Please share your #FamousOnTinderPS

CREATIVE METAPHORS

EXERCISE: Imagine creative metaphors for these concepts. Metaphors are potent shortcuts to instant and memorable understanding through comparison. A metaphor states that something is something else without using the word "like" or "as." They say this "is" that, "was" that or "are" that. It lets you transfer the qualities of one thing directly to another.

WHY?: Metaphors can evoke vivid images and allow us to "see" things from a new perspective. They are useful tools for creative problem-solving. Metaphors make your writing and speaking voice a lot more interesting, especially when they are poignant or funny, and using them is a unique challenge of your creative focus.

EXAMPLE:

LOVE IS... a battlefield.
- Pat Benatar

CONSCIENCE IS... a man's compass."
- Vincent Van Gogh

THE SUN WAS... a toddler insistently refusing to go to bed: It was past eight-thirty and still light.
- John Green

@pilgrim_soul_creative

CREATIVE METAPHORS

Hate is...

She was...

Free time is...

Traffic is...

Hunger is...

Sugar is...

Bank accounts are...

Possessions are...

Language is...

Deadlines are...

INTUITIVE CIRCLES

EXERCISE: This exercise was made famous by the design firm Ideo. Take 15 minutes to transform the circles into personal objects by adding visual elements (soccer ball, dinner plate, abstract art, etc.). Don't think about it too much, use your intuition and just let your drawing hand lead the way. Don't worry about quality.

WHY?: Creativity is about accessing your intuitive, instinctive mind. When generating ideas with quick, impulsive exercises, you are pursuing quantity more than quality. Quality will be there- it's inevitable if you let your mind crank out ideas. Your results will be even better if you train your brain to go to different, unpredictable places with your thinking. The key to this exemplary creative focus exercise is creating a lot of options for yourself- invariably, there will be gold among all of the rubble.

INTUITIVE CIRCLES

Please share your #IntuitiveCirclesPS

INTUITIVE CIRCLES

Please share your #IntuitiveCirclesPS

BENEFIT OF A BENEFIT

EXERCISE: Answer the prompt question, then take your answer and make it the next question. Keep doing this, in a chain, to 5 levels of questions. Don't jump too radically far in any one Q&A step; leave room for gradations/links along the way to the ultimate colossal benefit. And don't stop when you think you run out of benefits. Force yourself to keep going.

WHY?: You see where we're going with this, right? The point is to train your brain to keep digging and digging. At some point, your brain struggles. It's tempting to give up. This exercise helps you see things that are not readily apparent. It also teaches you to see the smaller links between the more significant ideas and to draw inferences, an essential skill in making creative connections.

EXAMPLE:

WHAT'S THE BENEFIT OF USING THIS JOURNAL?
It will help me to be more creative.

WHAT'S THE BENEFIT OF BEING MORE CREATIVE?
I will differentiate me from other people.

WHAT'S THE BENEFIT OF DIFFERENTIATING FROM OTHER PEOPLE?
It will demonstrate my unique talents - creating more and better work.

WHAT'S THE BENEFIT OF MORE AND BETTER WORK?
Make more money.

WHAT'S THE BENEFIT OF MORE MONEY?
More freedom to be creative and make an impact on this world.

THE BENEFIT OF A
Benefit

What is the benefit of being funny?

What is the benefit of being happy?

HELLO PROFESSOR

EXERCISE: You've done it - your unique expertise has been recognized, and now your people are clamoring to learn from you. Create a 'Class Overview' of something not often taught in schools that you want to teach. It could be anything,
- How To Win Arguments with Friends or lovers?
- Getting Out of Traffic Tickets 101?
- Or maybe, How to Procrastinate Online?
For your class, write out a Course Syllabus with descriptions of goals, classroom expectations, and required preparation.

WHY?: To teach effectively, professors structure their knowledge and formalize their instruction into an organized plan. Making a teaching plan for an unusual subject is a textbook exercise in creative focus. It requires you to take a mental inventory of what you know, and then to synthesize it into an accessible format. Explaining your unique knowledge in a relatable, deliberate curriculum for others to absorb, strengthens your own intellectual and creative abilities

CLASS CURRICULUM

Course Title:
Course Description:

Syllabus & Final Project:

Prerequisites:

Goals:	Class Rules:

Required course materials:

Homework Assignments:

CLASS CURRICULUM

Course Title:
Course Description:

Syllabus & Final Project:

Prerequisites:

Goals:	Class Rules:

Required course materials:

Homework Assignments:

Please share your #HelloProfessorPS

Please share your #AdultColoringPS

CONCISE COMPLAINTS

EXERCISE: Why are these people protesting? Restore our faith in complaints by imagining what these people are objecting to and giving them an attention-grabbing sign. Feel free to use metaphors or similes to add color. But remember - nobody likes an overly wordy protest sign.

WHY?: Complaining is one of the top creative outlets for unsatisfied people. Real-life often seems full of things you can't change. With verbal creativity, you can obtain more of a feeling of control over things that frustrate you. By exercising your own descriptive spin to create a beautiful, colloquial language out of something negative, it challenges your creative focus.

WHY ARE THESE PEOPLE
Protesting?

Please share #ConciseComaplaintsPS

89

WORD LINKS

EXERCISE: Connect the word on the left side of the page with its same-row word on the right side of the page by using four or five words in between to link them. Have each word build a bridge with a logical connection to the next. You should end up with a set of word links that get you from the first word to the last word in some obvious or surprising logic.

WHY?: It isn't easy to think unpredictably by looking in one direction. When your attention is focused on a single subject, limited and predictable patterns will dominate your thinking. By forcing relationships with things that are not related, different and unusual patterns are activated, which can be an invaluable exercise in creative focus.

EXAMPLE:

BUTTERFLY Bee Honey Sugar Carbohydrate Wheat **PIZZA**

WORD LINKS

TAMBOURINE _____ SQUIRREL

ELEPHANT _____ SPARK PLUG

PHILOSOPHER _____ PIZZA

HANDGUN _____ FLOWER

BEAUTY PAGEANT _____ HOT SAUCE

PICKLE _____ Q-TIP

FRUSTRATED _____ MARSHMALLOW

MULTIVITAMIN _____ STAR TREK

BARTENDER _____ OAK TREE

PICK UP TRUCK _____ PEANUT BUTTER

IPHONE _____ UNDERWEAR

SADNESS _____ PICKLE

WINE _____ EMBEZZLEMENT

TEENAGERS _____ CHICKENNUGGET

SUPERMAN _____ COUGH MEDICINE

SENATOR _____ DUCK

REMOTE CONTROL _____ DIVORCE

CITY SLOGANS

EXERCISE: Tourism is down in these cities, but you've got a winning solution to bring in visitors: A New Slogan! Create a city slogan in a very concise, snappy form. Share the positive (or funny) attributes of a place with the feelings attached. It can be serious, silly, whatever you like. Real examples of some state slogans include "Virginia Is For Lovers," "Maryland of Opportunity," "Vermont, Naturally." Of course, yours can be far funnier than any real one, if you like.

WHY?: Effective slogans are a perfect condensation of wit, description and enticement. Coming up with them requires apprehending diverse information and distilling down the essence in a way that "sells" the product in a split second, ideally makes people smile and simultaneously understand the value proposition and appreciate the linguistic artistry. Such an exercise involves pure creative focus.

EXAMPLE:

New York City

1. "George Washington Schlepped here"
2. "If you can make it there, you can't necessarily make it out of there"
3. " The City That Never Sweeps"

CITY SLOGANS

Miami, Florida

1.

2.

3.

CITY SLOGANS

Dallas, Texas

1.

2.

3.

Please share your #CitySlogansPS

CITY SLOGANS

Los Angeles, California

1.

2.

3.

Please share your #CitySlogansPS

VERTICAL POEMS

EXERCISE: In this exercise we'll use a "spine" word as the launching pad for your vertical poetry by writing words across starting each letter of the word. This is known as Acrostic poetry. It does not have to relate directly to what you are writing about, but it can. You can play with acoustics, explain what the word means to you, or describe how you see fit.

WHY?: Poetry, as opposed to prose, is writing with almost no format constraints. It's like an abstract painting with words. Yet, poetry not only helps the mind with creative, artistic thinking, it even helps with more technical endeavors. According to BioScience Magazine, "creativity- more specifically, poetry- helps scientists to communicate their work in compelling ways. It increases engagement and enhances learning." Using word triggers to build poems, helps hone your creative focus.

EXAMPLE:

> **R**ed is for
>
> **E**ntering
>
> **D**angerous poems

VERTICAL POEMS

T _____

H _____

I _____

N _____

K _____

V _____

O _____

T _____

E _____

C _____

A _____

T _____

S _____

VERTICAL POEMS

T _____

O _____

U _____

C _____

H _____

F _____

U _____

N _____

L _____

O _____

V _____

E _____

Please share your #VerticalPoemPS

Emphasize the flaws
Voice nagging suspicions
Think: Inside the work, outside the work
Humanize something free of error
Be less critical more often.

– **BRIAN ENO**,
Musician, Record Producer

THE 6-WORD STORY

EXERCISE: Let's play with brevity. For this exercise, create a story in just six words. You can do it. Focus on the essence of the narrative. Provide a movement of conflict, action, and resolution that gives the sense of a complete story transpiring in a moment's reading. Look at the examples below.

WHY?: Creativity often involves simplifying the complicated. Ernest Hemingway was one of many writers who created a six-word story as an example of concise and creative storytelling. "For sale: Baby shoes. Never worn." When you boil down the ingredients, you gain intensity, an exercise that captures the essence of a creative focus.

EXAMPLE:

Longed for him. Got him. Shit. **- MARGARET ATWOOD**

All those pages in the fire. **- JANET BURROWAY**

Goodbye mission control. Thanks for trying. **- ANONYMOUS**

Why are you in my selfie? **- ADAM GROPMAN**

@pilgrim_soul_creative

6-WORD STORIES

PEOPLE ANALOGIES

EXERCISE: Match a famous person of the past with a current notorious figure to make pairs of "People Analogies." Write in your complementing names of recent celebrities on the right for well-known people of the past. Then add a very brief explanation of what they have in common.

WHY?: Thinking in analogies helps to recognize patterns and types around the world and through time. They allow you to step between worlds that seem disconnected and connect them based on some structure to help you come up with new ideas. Specific characteristics are rarely ever brand new, our brain makes analogous comparisons unconsciously all the time, as a mode of creative focus and making sense of the world around us.

EXAMPLE:

FRANK SINATRA = Justin Timberlake
Both charismatic singers who crossed over into acting.

MUHAMMAD ALI = Lebron James
Highly principled, tell-it-like-it-is, represent the underdog and top of their sport

@pilgrim_soul_creative

PEOPLE ANALOGIES

BARBRA STREISAND –

AUDREY HEPBURN –

SELENA QUITANILLA –

STEVE MCQUEEN –

HOWARD HUGHES –

MARLON BRANDO –

ROBERT REDFORD –

HARRY BELAFONTE –

FARRAH FAWCETT –

And think of your <u>own</u> people analogies.

SEMIOTICS

EXERCISE: Go with your instinct here. Match the made-up word with a symbol to the right. Use each word and symbol once. Don't be arbitrary- feel your intuitive connection between the linguistic and symbolic.

WHY?: This exercise involves the semiotic relationship between words and symbols. Semiotics, defined as the study of signs and symbols and their use or interpretation, helps us intuitively connect the left analytical brain and the creative thinking right brain. The creative brain is engaged in this exercise through your pursuit of meaning, the sense you create behind communication, and the logical principles that structure our focused imagination.

SEMIOTICS

CHEVESIC

SKAXIS

LULERAIN

CRESTBOOT

VASAGLE

CASTREALM

LUEZOID

FEANDRA

XANPON

LOSENOID

Please share your #SemioticsPS

PLACE PERSONALITY

EXERCISE: Describe each of these places as if they are a person. Imagine the physical place itself, with its qualities and attributes, shrinks down into a human form. Don't limit yourself to simple - tall, short, fat, skinny, etc. but feel free to go into detail. What do they look like? How do they talk? Walk? What do they like to eat?

WHY?: Here we're asking for you to look beyond the surface and to find the underlying emotional and intrinsic values of a particular place. What is the essence of this place, and how can you convey that in a description that might even make you think of it differently? Pushing beyond linear and concrete concepts is an exercise rooted in creative focus because it forces you to reimagine a play or concept through its essence rather than its actual definition.

EXAMPLE:

CHICAGO PERSONALITY

A tall blocky guy named Logan. His voice has a resonant, low reed-instrument like sound, and he always somehow towers over you. He's an extrovert, open and friendly. Spends more time talking about sports than the weather. He loves hotdogs, never with ketchup. Will defend his pizza vs. New York's or any other city's pizza. If you get lost or need help, he's more than happy to give directions. Though he may ask, who senchya?

@pilgrim_soul_creative

PLACE PERSONALITY

NEW YORK

_____

TOKYO

Please share your #PlacePersonalityPS

PLACE PERSONALITY

WALMART

WALMART
STORES

PARIS

Please share your #PlacePersonalityPS

PLACE PERSONALITY

NEW ORLEANS

WHOLE FOODS

NEW IDIOMS

EXERCISE: Idioms are short phrases that have a very commonly known meaning different from their literal meaning. You can embed idioms in casual, colloquial speech, such as "a dime a dozen" or "beating a dead horse." Read the obscure or made up idiom and then explain its meaning. Write in a sentence.

WHY?: Idioms are a primally important part of any language. Humans take the formal content and structure of their native language and create another layer of phrases with colorful meanings to express ideas that may be difficult to adequately communicate with such flair and emotion otherwise. By involving your right brain with deciphering the relationship between idioms and their meaning, you are sharpening your creative focus.

EXAMPLE:

"Tilting the cat"

Making others uncomfortable, doing something on the brink of causing trouble.

NEW IDIOMS

"Like a dog in church."

"Dumplings instead of flowers."

"Jumping from a rain cloud to a rabbit."

"Emit smoke from seven orifices"

"Walk around in hot porridge."

"Selling pine cones in Patagonia."

"Hang noodles on someone's ears."

"Still riding the goat."

HOLLYWOOD PITCH

EXERCISE: You're a Hollywood producer and it's your big shot to pitch a film that you believe will be the next great picture. But the Studio Executives are having a hard time understanding what exactly your movie is. Think up 3 big Hollywood movies that are "this meets that," and then write a name and short blurb (called a 'logline' in the entertainment industry) describing the film.

WHY?: Einstein referred to this method of creative innovation as "Combinatory Play." It is - when two previously existing ideas are put together in a new way. For the movie business, in particular, a lot of creative work involves combining or synthesizing pre-existing elements. By actively merging two separate subjects into the same space, you articulate a new identity. This new identity will encourage you to think of connecting links and plausible circumstances to express them, thereby testing your creative focus.

EXAMPLE:

MOVIE NAME
Tagged

COMPARISON: Die Hard meets The Social Network
LOG-LINE: While on vacation in Silicon Valley, an off duty NYPD detective is mistakenly identified as an enemy of the state when he is unwittingly tagged in a terrorist's selfie. While being hunted by the CIA, he works to clear his name and foil the plot.

@pilgrim_soul_creative

THE HOLLYWOOD PITCH

MOVIE NAME

COMPARISON:
LOG-LINE:

MOVIE NAME

COMPARISON:
LOG-LINE:

MOVIE NAME

COMPARISON:
LOG-LINE:

Please share your #HollywoodPitchPS

HUMAN ZOO

EXERCISE: Imagine your local coffee shop as a Human Zoo, where you can observe and interact with the animals in their natural habitat. Write a field guide for future visitors, describing the human types commonly encountered there.

WHY?: A field guide is a rather technical, descriptive reference book cataloging all of the animals, objects, terrain, etc. that one will find in a given environment. The most commonly known type of field guide covers birds of a given setting. Writing a field guide requires expertise, descriptive abilities, organizational structure, and, of course, a good deal of creative awareness.

COFFEE SHOP
Field Guide

Name (real or imagined):

Distinctive Markings:

Sounds they make:

Life Span:

Natural Predators / Prey:

Visual Description:

Social Habits:

Natural Habitat:

Diet:

Special Skills:

MY TALK SHOW

EXERCISE: You're the host of a popular late-night TV talk show and your guests, rather than celebrities, are the everyday people you come into contact with. Think of 3 interview questions for these 3 people that delves into the most thought - provoking aspects of their routine lives.

"EVERYONE IS INFINITELY INTERESTING FOR 15 MINUTES?"
- Ondi Timoner, Documentary Filmmaker

WHY?: As aspiring creatives, we often want to create brilliant things from scratch. But a valid branch of art is finding and repurposing or plugging in existing elements that we see in our travels. This is what collage artists, documentarians, and modern DJ's do. By thinking of compelling questions for everyday people, we activate our empathy and curiosity, gaining an appreciation for nuance, which develops our creative awareness.

EXAMPLE:
AMAZON PRIME DELIVERY GUY

1.) Do you feel you can get to know someone by the type of packages they receive? How so?

2.) You ever open something out of curiosity and seal it back up?

3.) What's the most surprising thing you've seen when someone answers the door?

@pilgrim_soul_creative

MY TALK SHOW GUESTS

GARBAGE MAN
(the person who empties the garbage cans)

Interview Questions

1.

2.

3.

FAST FOOD DRIVE-THROUGH PERSON
(the person who hands you your meal)

Interview Questions

1.

2.

3.

PAID SUPERMARKET CHARITY FUNDRAISER
(the person who stands outside the exit with a clipboard)

Interview Questions

1.

2.

3.

Please share your #MyTalkShowPS

VERY SPECIFIC PLAYLIST

EXERCISE: Set the musical mood by creating the playlist for a gathering of different types of people. This group could be anyone - Beauty Influencers, Car Salesman, Railroad Conductors, Bike Couriers, Feng Shui Consultants, or Headhunters. Use your open, associative mind to make a connection with the songs which don't have to be literal. It can be about a universal feel, theme, or vibe, as well as the actual direct words.

WHY?: This exercise involves categorizing items from an inventory (songs) while also making leaps of thought, using your intuitive sense. Not every song will necessarily have the same type of criteria for inclusion in a specific group's playlist. As the DJ, you will make creative leaps, connecting a given song to an affiliation based on multiple layers of association. This kind of exercise strengthens the sector of your brain used for differentiating, arranging, and curating lists of items around often abstract themes. It's a calculating creative focus workout.

VERY SPECIFIC
Playlists

AUDIENCE

Instagram Influencers

Songs

1.
2.
3.
4.
5.

AUDIENCE

Songs

1.
2.
3.
4.
5.

AUDIENCE

Songs

1.
2.
3.
4.
5.

Please share your #VerySpecificPlaylistPS

SUBJECTIVE MAP

EXERCISE: Create a handwritten map of an imaginary neighborhood or planned community, with an overlay showing destinations and amenities relevant to a specific group, such as Hipsters, Boring People, Hypochondriacs, Narcissists, Narcoleptics, your dog, you pick.

WHY?: According to National Geographic, spatial thinking is one of the most critical formative mental skills, one that's required for interaction with the world. Spatial thinking involves visualizing, interpreting, and reasoning, using location, distance, direction, and space. This exercise, combining mapping skills with sociological and anthropological observation, uses both the scientific left brain and creative right brain. It fosters creative awareness while also helping us to realize our own social biases.

Man's Man Neighborhood Map

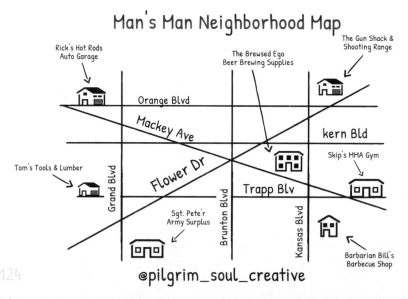

@pilgrim_soul_creative

PLANNED COMMUNITY
for:

JUNK MAIL REVIEW

EXERCISE: Write a Yelp style review for a piece of junk mail that you've recently received. Somebody was actually paid to write it, and you're a critic, when you choose to open it or throw it away. Be creative and open-minded, reviewing the various relevant criteria. How successful was the copywriter in their attempt at seduction, emotional selling, solving problems, appealing to desire, and establishing credibility? Leave no detail spared as you warn or excite the world about this piece of junk. And don't forget to leave a star rating!

WHY?: What if we look at things in a completely different way? There are things for which we feel it's reasonable to write a user review. But what if we wrote a user review for an everyday item we detest or ignore? Thinking about things we take for granted, like the purpose of this document, opens us up to creative awareness.

@pilgrim_soul_creative

JUNK MAIL REVIEW

PRODUCT / SERVICE

HEADLINE:

ENVELOPE:

CALL TO ACTION:

BENEFIT:

EMOTIONAL APPEAL:

VALUES:

GRAPHICS:

RATING (fill in 1-5):

Please share your #JunkMailReviewPS

LOVE INSTRUCTIONS

EXERCISE: Could it be that falling in love is as simple as following a set of instructions? Write a guide for how to meet and convince someone to fall in love with you. And like a good instruction manual, please assume your user has never done this before. Highlight the essential tools you'll need for assembly. Define where the set of procedures starts and finishes and what problems a user may encounter during its execution. You can make it truthful or satirical; just make sure that in the end, the task can actually be completed.

WHY?: There is a whole field of "technical writing," which addresses product documentation and user manuals. This kind of left - brain writing requires very functional logic and clarity. It is the antithesis of creativity. By applying this template to a non - technical, right - brain topic, you force your brain into a new area of hybrid reasoning, thereby building on your creative awareness.

EXAMPLE:

INSTRUCTIONS FOR BEING LIKED AT A POKER GAME

AUDIENCE: Novice Player
TOOLS NEEDED: Cash, Food, Humility
AUTHOR: P. Soul

STEPS

1. Bring sandwiches, chips and beer.
2. Call out the cleverness of other players when you deal.
3. Lose a bunch of money early on.

A PRACTICAL GUIDE

 to Finding Love

AUDIENCE:

TOOLS NEEDED:

AUTHOR:

<u>STEPS</u>

1.

2.

3.

4.

5.

6.

7.

8.

BIG QUESTIONS

EXERCISE: Here are some big questions - answer them without thinking. Really. Don't stop and think of what the best answer might be, or the expected response. Just reply with the first ideas that flow through your mind.

WHY?: We tend to think of questions and answers as linear, exact, and technical. We expect every problem to be narrowly confined and every answer to be defensible by conventional logic. And this leads us to question a process before we've even completed it. That is analogous to driving with one foot on the brake and one on the accelerator. By breaking out of our regular thought limitations to spur creative ideation, and bring a sense of fun and unpredictable insight into our ideas.

ANSWER THESE
BIG QUESTIONS

1. What is something that everyone looks stupid doing?

2. If animals could talk, which would be the rudest?

3. In one sentence, how would you sum up the internet?

Please share your #BigQuestionsPS

ANSWER THESE
BIG QUESTIONS

4. What are the sexiest and least sexy names?

5. What are some fun and interesting alternatives to war that countries could settle their differences with?

ANSWER THESE
BIG QUESTIONS

6. If you were transported 400 years into the past with no clothes or anything else, how would you prove that you were from the future?

7. How many Chickens would it take to kill an elephant? Why so?

NEW ADMISSIONS

EXERCISE: You are Head of Admissions for a progressive University, and they've asked you to conceive an entirely new system for admitting students - no SAT's or ACT's, no grades, no transcripts. List some of your groundbreaking new criteria for admitting students.

WHY?: Thinking analytically and in terms of innovative criteria for finding cases of distinction and quality helps sharpen the brain. In many jobs and endeavors, finding real talent and strong character is of the utmost importance, and using out - of - the - box creativity in filtering applicants can often yield the most successful results. Solving the very real-world problems with unusual solutions exercises your creative awareness.

EXAMPLE:

COLLEGE ADMISSIONS TEST

Put the applicant in a cocktail party or small group setting, where there's conversing, and observe/listen to them.

COLLEGE ADMISSIONS
A New Approach

Please share your #NewAdmissionsPS

TWO KINDS OF PEOPLE

EXERCISE: Think of and write down 6 fun, useful binary criteria by which to classify and separate people. Whether beneficial or ridiculous, Share how it could be helpful to you or anyone. Oscar Wilde wrote, "There's no such thing as good or bad, people are either charming or tedious." Maybe that's not entirely true for everyone, but it served as a useful classification for the people Oscar wanted to spend time with.

WHY?: Social categorization refers to the way a person's brain groups together individuals who share essential characteristics. According to psychologist Galen Bodenhausen, this process allows people to organize and structure their understanding of the social world, and make sense of the complex, multifaceted environment around them, thereby activating their creative awareness.

EXAMPLE:

THOSE WHO PREFER CATS VS. DOGS

Dog owners are the most fun to be with. Cat owners are the most dependable and emotionally sensitive.
Dog people wish their dogs were people.
Cat people wish they were cats.

@pilgrim_soul_creative

THERE ARE TWO
Kinds of People

1. Those who...

2. Those who...

3. Those who...

4. Those who...

5. Those who...

6. Those who...

CREATIVE NAPPING

EXERCISE: In this exercise, we'll utilize a powerful tool: which is sleep. Sit in a comfortable chair and take a short nap while holding your keys in your hand. When you fall asleep, the keys will hit the ground, waking you up. As soon as you wake up, write down any ideas you can remember. There is a moment when our brains are at a midpoint between conscious and unconscious, right before you fall asleep when ideas solidify, and you wake up with fully formed answers to a previously unsolved problem.

WHY?: Thomas Edison would do this by holding ball bearings in his hand as he fell asleep, and the noise of them falling to the floor would wake him immediately, generating the shortest possible power nap. After this, he would go right back to inventing. Salvador Dali did the same with cutlery and his art. The imagination is powerful during sleep. Naps, along with procrastination, can sometimes be integral to the creative process. Our subconscious goes to work dreaming up ideas. In dreams, we think differently, and our brains are unharnessed from daily routines. We condense, rearrange, amplify, and combine things in ways that we rarely do when awake.

CREATIVE NAPPING
Ideas

NOT WANTED POSTER

EXERCISE: Create a "wanted" style poster about a person you think is a jerk. Someone you resent or dislike, who wronged or slighted you, toward whom you may have a bit have animosity. Make it about character development. Build a "most wanted" style character around their persona, like George "Machine Gun" Kelly or "Baby Face" Nelson.

WHY?: This thought experiment can be very cathartic as you get to externalize your feelings and assessments of this person in a fun and creative manner. Breaking down the person's qualities into colorful, descriptive details is a form of gossip. Research from Queen's University in Belfast shows that gossip and creativity share the same cognitive resources, and can be experimentally manipulated using a dual-task paradigm. When you apply your observational and descriptive mind and engage in the act of colorful gossip, you are also participating in a creative awareness exercise.

NOT WANTED POSTER

Name and Nickname:

Why:

Build:

Height:

Weight:

Hair Color:

Eye color:

Nationality:

Last seen wearing:

Occupation:

Distinguishing marks:

Caution:

CAT NAMES

EXERCISE: Oh no ! Your worst fears have come to light and you're living alone with all 9 cats that you've collected. But they sure are adorable. What are their names? Share 9 of your favorite cat names.

WHY?: We all know the naming of cats is a peculiar thing. It requires an understanding of personality, relatability, disposition and whimsy. Cat names are personal, both to the owner and to the creature itself. Understanding link of the name and the underlying characters of the animal is an excellent exercise of creative awareness.

EXAMPLE:

CELEBRITY CAT NAMES

Cat Benatar	Cat Sajak
Catalie Portman	Donald Tramp
Cindy Clawford	Jude Paw
Meowly Cyrus	Notorious C.A.T
Pawdrey Hepburn	William Shakespaw

YOU OWN 9 CATS.
What are their names?

1. _____   4. _____   7. _____

2. _____   5. _____   8. _____

3. _____   6. _____   9. _____

Please share your #MyCatPS

PENMANSHIP PERSONALITY

EXERCISE: Write this note: "Hello! I stopped by. How are you?" over again, using the handwriting of various types of people. Try to capture the personality and mentality of each kind of person with your handwriting, and make them all really distinct. Feel free to utilize very different sizes, curvatures, neatness/messiness, dots/crosses, or whatever creative elements come to mind regarding the letters.

WHY?: Graphology, the science of analyzing handwriting for personality traits, has been around since the ancient Greeks. It is used today in criminology, medical science, and even human resources. Small details in someone's handwriting can reveal up to 5,000 personality traits. Tapping into the correlation between handwriting and inner personality, and imagining how others may write, combines empathy and artistry for a powerful exercise in creative focus.

PENMANSHIP
Personality

Hello! I stopped by. How are you?

A Rap artist from the early 1980's

HELLO! I STOPPED BY. HOW ARE YOU?

Psychopath Serial Murderer

Giggly 14 Year Old Girl Who Loves Horses

Scientific Prodigy Genius Who's Solving Physics Problems

Please Share Your #PenmanshipPS

PENMANSHIP
Personality

Hello! I stopped by. How are you?

Long Time Marine Drill Sergeant With No Other Interests

Bon Vivant Socialite Who Does Oil Painting For Fun

Gentle Pothead Who Works In a Tollbooth
& Reads Adult Comic Books

Very Busy Professional Mom With 3 Kids

Please Share Your #PenmanshipPS

Please share your #AdultColoringPS

SPORTY SOMMELIER

EXERCISE: You are a connoisseur of sports. Take each of the terms on the right, commonly used as adjectives and attributes for wine, and re-apply them to sports and athletes. Write a new, contextual sports definition for each and use in a sentence.

WHY?: Wine tasting culture is admired and ridiculed for its colorful and sometimes silly adjectives. But they have created a wonderfully expressive and compelling vernacular for an often subtle and complex phenomenon. By using this terminology to create your own lexicon for an entirely different subject - sports fandom - you are testing your creative awareness.

EXAMPLE:

The wine term "Spicy" refers to how it smells like various spices, ranging from pepper to cinnamon, to 5 spice or cloves.

NEW SPORTS USE

SPICY
Unpredictable, innovative, out - of - the - box play. Can extend to on/off - field personality. "Shawn Hopkins isn't the strongest 2nd baseman on paper, but he's spicy, he gets his own team riled up, and gets in the head of opposing base runners."

@pilgrim_soul_creative

SPORTY SOMMELIER
What is the sports reference?

FRUITY

ACIDITY

LEGS

BOUQUET

LEAFY

BRUT

MUSICAL SKETCHING

EXERCISE: Before you start this exercise - cue up
MOZART'S, EINE KLEINE NACHTMUSIK on your favorite
device. Hit play on your device and sit back. Close your eyes.
Really listen to the music intently. Hear its flow and rise. It's
fall and crests. Then, after two minutes, draw what you hear.
Don't feel the need to draw with an exact intention, just let
your pen move freely.

WHY?: It is not just about what you draw but also about
engaging your brain differently. The painter Wassily Kandinsky
is famous for listening to music while he would work. His music
choice would directly inform his canvases, and he noted it was
integral to his process. He did this because the practice engaged
his entire brain. If you're only listening, you're only activating
one part of the brain, But if you are drawing while listening,
you begin to allow yourself to make deeper, kinesthetic
connections between the music, your environment, and the
canvas. Music, as we're using it in this exercise, triggers the
release of neurotransmitters such as dopamine, serotonin, and
norepinephrine, which helps you feel relaxed, happy,
and creative.

SKETCHING
Mozart's Eine Kleine Nachtmusik

SPECIAL OCCASION BANDS

EXERCISE: You're an event producer with a diverse set of clients. Take this list of events and hire a band to play the event that you feel has the required "musical feel" and image to be appropriate for the occasion. Name the music group or performer's name that would be appropriate to perform at the specific event or occasion, and the signature song they'd play.

WHY?: Thinking across the divide from life events to musical styles requires an ability to intuitively sense the appropriateness of the artistic expression to the sensibility of the event and audience. Great DJ's know how to read a room and guide its vibe with their song selection. To do this, they incorporate empathy, knowledge, and intuition. To Successfully match music with the essential elements of an event is a prime example of creative awareness.

EXAMPLE:

DIVORCE PARTY:
Fleetwood Mac, Go Your Own Way

PLUMBERS CONVENTION:
The Strokes, Meet Me In The Bathroom

SPECIAL
OCCASION BANDS

THE FUNERAL FOR "BAMBI'S MOM."

THE GRAND PREMIERE OF THE NEWEST REVOLUTIONARY
NO-STICK FRYING PAN.

A WELCOME PARTY FOR SPACE
ALIENS ON OUR PLANET.

THE OPENING OF THE CHESS GRANDMASTER
CHAMPIONSHIP MATCH.

THE WEDDING OF THE STARS OF TWO SEPARATE VERY
SHALLOW, SENSATIONALISTIC REALITY TV SHOWS.

COMING OUT PARTY FOR A CHAMPION
MMA CHAMPIONSHIP FIGHTER.

Please share your #OccasionBandsPS

TINY HEADLINE

EXERCISE: Think of something seemingly small and insignificant that happened to you and write about it in the style of a front-page newspaper article. Blow it out of proportion. Use as few words as possible to grab our attention. And give a bit of the story to really make the mundane moment in your life extraordinary and relatable.

WHY?: Both fiction and journalism require writers to present scenarios efficiently and with razor clarity. By taking something seemingly small and insignificant in your life and writing about it as if it's essential "news," you will be stretching your perception, and expressive skills. Writing journalistically in this way requires that you search for the political, social, economic, and other ramifications of an event, expanding your creative awareness of your life and your world.

EXAMPLE:

HUSBAND REFUSES TO DO DISHES

Casper Meyer is perhaps the world's laziest man. He wasn't always that way. He dreamed of grand achievements - he was an energetic young man filled with dreams, who achieved high marks at university. He had an answer to every problem and was the first to volunteer to lend a hand. Now, he can't even get up from the couch.

@pilgrim_soul_creative

TINY HEADLINE

DAILY ⚛ NEWS

TINY HEADLINE

DAILY☙NEWS

Please share your #TinyHeadlinePS

Please share your #AdultColoringPS

UN-INVENTIONS

EXERCISE: Taking a page out of the revisionist history book. You invented a company that un-invents things that currently exist. What are your top un-inventions, and why? What do you dislike about these inventions?

WHY?: A lot of creative work is ultimately editing. Removing the parts of the story, sculpture, song, or movie that detracts from the creation's full potential. Likewise, on a larger scale, imagining a world without a particular technology or experience is a form of editing and a useful workout for the brain. Imagining the surrounding world being altered and re-ordered by the absence of said phenomenon broadens your spectrum of creative awareness.

EXAMPLE:

LEAF BLOWERS: What's wrong with rakes? Do we really need to clean up and pollute the air at the same time?

SWAG: If you have to boast that you have it, you probably don't.

UN-INVENTIONS

1.

2.

3.

4.

5.

4:20 OF LISTENING

EXERCISE: Go to a place, preferably outdoors, where you can sit or stand comfortably, and set a timer for 4 mins, 20 seconds. During that time, listen and take in everything you hear. After, write down what you heard. What did you become aware of? What came into your consciousness about your surroundings that you usually are unaware of?

THE QUIETER YOU BECOME, THE MORE YOU ARE ABLE TO HEAR.
– Rumi

WHY?: Our senses attain another level of perception and perspective when we allow ourselves to enter a calm, meditative state of pure sensory intake. Just as the slight ambient light in your nighttime bedroom seems to increase as your pupils widen, and you see more details, your ability to hear sounds opens up when you take the time to really listen. This is a simple yet poignant lesson in creative awareness.

4:20 OF LISTENING

VIBING

EXERCISE: Think of all the different kinds of places you visit in your day-to-day life then Write down a shortlist of places that make you feel a certain way. Share a short description of why each site makes you feel the way it does.

WHY?: Locations have always been central to human thought and feeling. Anthropologists have found that in traditional societies, the memory becomes attached to places. Places make us feel specific ways because of the social context, the physical setting, and past associations we may have. Becoming aware of how places affect us, and what qualities, strengths, and weaknesses, they tend to bring out makes our minds more aware and observant. Places sir up both external and internal realities, and provided a test of creative awareness.

@pilgrim_soul_creative

WHAT PLACE MAKES YOU FEEL THIS WAY?

1. Socially Confident

2. Wary

3. Melancholy

4. Angry

5. Peaceful

Please share your #VibingPS

PARTY SUBTEXT

EXERCISE: What are these party-goers really thinking? Take into account all of the things that can impact what they say and what they do. Do they have a secret? What external pressures are they facing? What is their mission? This will help you write their words and behavior with the underlying subtext driving the plot in this room.

WHY?: The subtext is the implicit meaning of a text. It gives the reader information about characters, plot, and the story's context as a whole. Great fiction writers and even non-fiction writers weave subtext through their work to communicate an underlying emotion and motives. It makes their prose richer and their dialogue more nuanced.

FILL IN THE
Thought Bubbles To Make This Office Party More Honest

Please share your #PartySubtextPS

FILL IN THE
Thought Bubbles To Make This Dinner with Friends More honest

Please share your #PartySubtextPS

FILL IN THE
Thought Bubbles To Make This Family Party More Honest

SNARKY COMMENTS

EXERCISE: Imagine you live in your mom's basement and spend your days writing snarky comments from your anonymous Instagram account. What kind of negative comments can you say about these commonly loved subjects?

WHY?: A study from the Harvard Business School suggests that blurting out sarcastic remarks-and listening to them-may increase one's ability to think creatively and abstractly. Sarcasm increases creativity for both expressers and recipients. Because you have to peel back the layers of the satirical remarks, your brain forces itself to analyze and interpret different possible meanings behind the comments - increasing ingenuity and creative problem-solving skills.

WHAT'S THERE TO BE CYNICAL ABOUT?

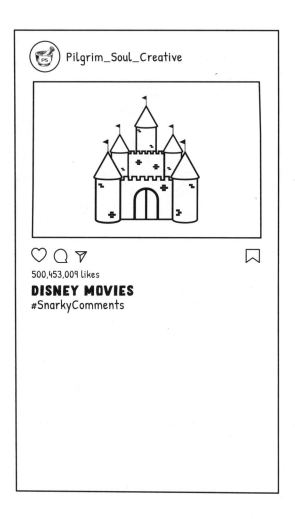

Pilgrim_Soul_Creative

500,453,009 likes

DISNEY MOVIES
#SnarkyComments

Please share your #SnarkyCommentsPS

WHAT'S THERE TO BE CYNICAL ABOUT?

Pilgrim_Soul_Creative

90,221,007 likes

BEING PRESENT
#SnarkyComments

Please share your #SnarkyCommentsPS

WHAT'S THERE TO BE CYNICAL ABOUT?

Pilgrim_Soul_Creative

1,2202,0229,109 likes

BABY ANIMALS
#SnarkyComments

BAND NAMES

EXERCISE: You're an A&R Exec at a hot new record label. Based on the descriptions of these bands, make up a memorable name for them. The best music groups often have names that are catchy and create an association in your mind, matching the bands' sound and look. Think about selling tickets and SWAG.

WHY?: Naming a music group stimulates the part of our brain where literal meets figurative, where the sound and feel of the word are as important as the meaning - and where the visual look of the name plays into its effectiveness, with such consideration as fonts, colors, stylized motifs and accompanying logo. This kind of brainstorming is a whimsical exercise in creative focus.

EXAMPLE:

NIRVANA

Nirvana got its name when they were tossing around goofy names like "Pen Cap Chew" and "Ted Ed Fred" when vocalist and guitarist Kurt Cobain said they should go with something beautiful instead of raunchy or aggressive. They managed to choose one of the most beautiful words ever created and made history with it.

@pilgrim_soul_creative

BAND NAMES

_____

Cuban American pop rock band from Florida with a flamboyantly dressed female lead singer.

_____

Hardcore speed metal band with two bassists, an extremely large drum set, and a growling lead singer, who performs live at about 15 decibels higher than most groups.

_____

Rap/Hip Hop group composed of 3 little people who have criminal records from gang involvement and can sing very melodic.

_____

A modern classical quartet of 2 cellos, a violin, and a trumpet, which specialize in creative, almost unrecognizable versions of classic rock hits.

_____

A neo-hippie jam band with 7 members- 2 keyboardists, 3 guitarists, drummer, and bass, who dress in kilts over psychedelic tights and Crocs on their feet. They play 15-minute songs.

_____

A tight, catchy jazzy quarter of singers doing vocal-heavy numbers with light instrumentation behind them, featuring a lot of harmonies, hand-off parts, and some vocal acrobatics, with cute, theatrical lyrics.

ELEVATOR ICE BREAKERS

EXERCISE: List your top 5 elevator tension breakers and tension makers. Be creative and funny, but share the situational psychology in which you'd say these things. As an example, you could say, "I thought they'd never leave," after someone gets off an elevator, as a way to make a personal connection with the people still riding along with you. I mean, nothing so fortifies a friendship as a mutual enemy.

WHY?: Framing the situation and thinking about what is really happening at the moment are essential building blocks of creativity. According to Deepak Chopra, talking to strangers in elevators brings with it a favorable aspect of random chance, enabling you to meet people you'd never meet. It also helps you stay in the moment and not retreat into your Smartphone or get caught up in obsessive ruminations. However, it is an awkward place to practice friendly "small talk," and to be effective and comfortable doing this requires creative awareness and empathy.

ELEVATOR ICE BREAKERS

CREATIVE REFLECTION

GENDER PERSPECTIVE

EXERCISE: Put yourself in the position of the opposite sex. Close your eyes and imagine that you are in the following settings, giving time for each one, EXCEPT - you are of the opposite gender. Place yourself there physically, mentally, psychologically. What do you notice that you normally would not? What are your thoughts and viewpoints, your feelings and reactions?

WHY?: Empathy begins with attention and awareness. Creativity does too. In both cases, you pay attention to the data you take in. In Latin, attention means to "stretch toward." When you empathize with someone, you're stretching outside of yourself and stretching into that person's world. This empathy then links to problem-solving because you must first decide not only what the problem is, but who has the problem, and in what context? This makes our minds more aware and observant. Places sir up both external and internal realities, and provided a test of creative awareness.

HOW I WOULD FEEL
If I were a Man/Woman (circle opposite gender)
In This Situation...

Wearing a bathing suit on a public beach...

Asking your boss for a raise...

Flirting and dancing at a party...

When the check arrives on your first date...

Ending a relationship that consisted of 3 dates...

Please share your #GenderPerspectivePS

PRIME VOICES

EXERCISE: The best thing a parent or teacher can do for a child is to believe in them. Take a moment and think of the profound and transcendent things that different people told you while growing up. It can be an original piece of advice that was shared or a quote they always repeated, that pertained to you. Something that resonated with you and affected you, positive or negative, that you still think about today.

WHY?: Positive reinforcement has always shown to have a positive output. If your parents told you you were creative, you increased your creative production and became more creative. The opposite is also true. Very often, our creativity is ruled by self-perceptions in our subconscious. It's like an inner newsreel we play back of people's reactions to us. Bringing these things forward is an act of creative reflection that will help you to understand your imposed inhibitions and open you up to creative freedom.

EXAMPLE:

> When I was 5 years old I told my mom
> that I wanted to grow up and be a musician.
> She said, "Sorry, honey, you can't do both."

PRIME VOICES

Positive Prime Voices

Negative Prime Voices

BACK FROM THE FUTURE

EXERCISE: If you want to work on your art, work on your life. Write a letter from yourself at 80 to your current self. Describe yourself at 80. What did you do after 50 that you enjoyed? What would you tell yourself? What interests would you urge yourself to pursue? What dreams would you encourage?

WHY?: People often think that creativity is based on fantasy. The truth is, creativity is about understanding who you are and getting past the fear. Self-expression requires a self to express. As we get precise about our life, we become more available to the moment. We become original because we become specific, an outcome this exercise fosters through creative reflection.

EXAMPLE:

ADVICE FROM MY 80 YEAR OLD SELF

Take the stairs every chance you get. When you get to be my age, taking the stairs is a privilege but you have to earn it by taking the stairs a lot throughout your life.

Only wear clothes that you love. You might die in what you're wearing so you should want it to be fabulous.

Make friends of all ages so there will be lots of young people around you when you're old. Don't limit your friendships to people you have everything in common with or who are the same age as you. Diversify your portfolio.

@pilgrim_soul_creative

A LETTER FROM
My 80 Year Old Self

How old are you now?

Describe yourself at 80?

What did you do after 50 that you enjoyed?
Be very specific.

A LETTER FROM
My 80 Year Old Self

Write a letter from you at eighty to your current self.

Dear Me,

Please share your #BackFromTheFuturePS

Don't think about making art, just get it done.
Let everyone else decide if it's good or bad,
whether they love it or hate it. While they
are deciding, make even more art.

– ANDY WARHOL,
Artist, Film Director

5.0 STAR PASSENGER

EXERCISE: Ensure your rider rating remains pristine. Write a thank you letter to your rideshare driver. Be effusive and descriptive in your appreciation. Think about the efficiency of the route and the smoothness of the car ride. The personality/behavior of the driver, the atmosphere, and the little extras inside the car. Share your empathy for his journey to that moment when you met.

WHY?: When you are grateful, you reduce your stress, and everyone involved experiences positive emotions. This also helps you to remember peripheral details more vividly, think outside the box, and recognize common themes among random or unassociated ideas. All of these add up to more creative responses. Research consistently shows that positive emotions broaden an individual's thought-action repertoire, which expands that individual's intellectual and social resources.

EXAMPLE:

"Dear Uber Driver,- Thank you! Your car smelled like bubblegum and rum spice aftershave- it reminded me of when I was 12 and used to drive with my dad. I wouldn't have chosen the "Finnish Psy Trance" music you played, but it exposed me to a whole new genre. I really appreciated the tiny bottle of water you gave me and marveled in how you could make a left turn across 4 lanes of traffic during rush hour, Bravo to you!"

@pilgrim_soul_creative

RIDESHARE DRIVER
Gratitude Letter

MY SITCOM

EXERCISE: Hollywood's calling again. This time they want you to make a sitcom about your life. It can be about you or someone you know. All they need from you is the Show's Name, a brief description, its slogan and your catchphrase. Write the name and slogan of the sitcom based on your life and the repeated catchphrase of your character.

WHY?: Sitcoms define characters and worlds in an exaggerated, colorful, yet condensed manner. The quirks and qualities of character are drawn broadly and shown explicitly, which enables the viewer to laugh at the use and manipulation of different archetypes. By using your own life as the basis for these sitcom elements, you sharpen your skills at distilling the facts and self-perception of your own life into their most essential, which adds up to a revealing exercise in creative reflection.

EXAMPLE:

SHOW NAME: The Cannabis Society

BRIEF DESCRIPTION: The daily life and interactions of an unusually successful stoner.

SLOGAN: "High, Society."

CATCHPHRASE: "But how High?"

@pilgrim_soul_creative

SITCOMS IN MY LIFE

Show Name:

Brief Description:

Slogan:

Catchphrase:

Show Name:

Brief Description:

Slogan:

Catchphrase:

Show Name:

Brief Description:

Slogan:

Catchphrase:

MY LIFE LIMERICK

EXERCISE: Write a limerick about yourself. Try to make it specific and real to your history or qualities. A limerick is a humorous poem that is often vulgar, in five-line, mostly anapestic meter, with the rhyme scheme AABBA. The 1st, 2nd, and 5th lines rhyme, while the 3rd and 4th lines are short and share a separate verse.

WHY?: Specific poetic formats-haiku, sonnet, ode, etc.- put a set of limits on a writer, which often results in an imaginative, highly disciplined work of art. Having constraints and a particular structure in the making of a work of art is constructive for many artists. It frees up the mind to fill in the spaces which require inspired content, thereby causing an instance of creative reflection.

EXAMPLE:

There once was a runner named Dwight
Who could speed even faster than light.
He set out one day / In a relative way
And returned on the previous night.

There was a young lady named Rose,
Who had a large wart on her nose.
When she had it removed,
Her appearance improved,
But her glasses slipped down to her toes.

A LIMERICK ABOUT
My Life

MY MIND MAP

EXERCISE: Draw a fun cartoon style map of your own mind. Think of all the different sides of your personality, emotions, and thoughts, and show them creatively using the terminology and imagery of those playful, colorful maps you might see at a tourist shop.

WHY?: Charts and maps often help to illuminate the relationship between disparate things that fall under a category umbrella. Engaging the visual side of our brain helps us to get a valuable new perspective on things we think we already know. Just thinking about who you are and what you feel, then expressing it visually, stimulates new depths of creative reflection.

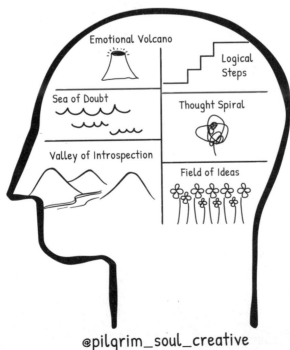

@pilgrim_soul_creative

MY MIND MAP

Please share your #MindMapPS

MY BIG IDEAL

EXERCISE: Come up with the "Big Ideal." for your personal brand. In one circle, you have **CULTURAL TENSION** that you are aware of - This is what is happening in the world that's relevant to you. In the other circle, **IS YOUR BEST SELF** - This is what you offer the world when you are in your zone. The intersection of these two areas is **'YOUR BIG IDEAL'** — or your creative purpose. Your goal is to land on one primary statement for each circle. Taken together, they should help inform how you complete the following sentence: "For (your name) the world would be a better place if _____."

WHY?: Ogilvy and Mather Advertising created this formula for brands to define their unique purpose and thrive as a brand. Use this formula to find your personal brand and creative focus, and to understand how you can make the world a better place. It's the intersection between what people care about what you could be famous for in your work. It is an eye-opening exercise in creative reflection and a recipe for doing something good that matters.

EXAMPLE: Dove Soap

Beauty anxiety is an age of Photoshop

Gentle alternative to soap that delivers real care

For Dove, the world would be a better place if
WOMEN WERE ALLOWED TO FEEL GOOD ABOUT THEIR BODIES.

202

@pilgrim_soul_creative

Cultural Tension   My Best Self

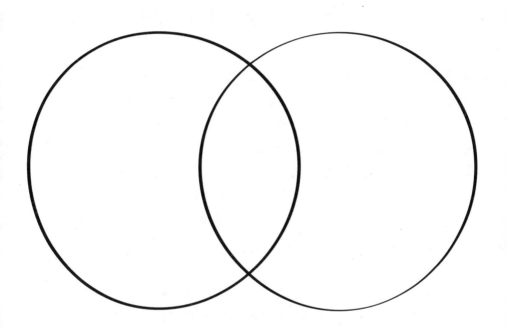

My Big Ideal

For _____ the world would be a better place if...

I AM

EXERCISE: "I am" are two of the most powerful words in the English language - what follows them creates your reality. You are who you think you are and affirmations are a proven tool for changing thought patterns and beliefs. Follow the specific self-talk directions on the right.

WHY?: According to Gregory Jantz, Ph.D., writing in Psychology Today, "Each of us has a set of messages that play over and over in our minds. This internal dialogue, or personal commentary, frames our reactions to life and its circumstances." He also talks about the importance of positive self-talk, and its ability to bring your life into productivity, stability and joy. We can "overwrite" the negative messages originally spoken by others in childhood, says Jantz, with new positive ones. When author and pastor Chuck Swindoll says that 10% of life is about what happens and the rest is how you react to it, he's talking about the power of positive self-talk as opposed to the negative variety. Thinking in this constructive way is a prime test of creative reflection.

MY SELF TALK

What have you been telling yourself about you lately?

What do you want to tell yourself? Write 4 things to tell yourself daily?

MY LIFE SCRIPT

EXERCISE: let's frame the movie of your life. Write the plot of your life story in bullet points following the arc outline used by many screenwriters. Outline each element and finally come up with the title of the movie of your life. What do you want your life to be, and how will you structure towards that?

WHY?: Film scripts follow a definite structure, with set plot occurrences and turning points at specific points within the text. By looking realistically and introspectively at your own life, and then conforming specific significant incidents and changes to the essential structure of a film script, you can't help but engage in creative reflection.

EXAMPLE:

Title:
Free Hand

SETUP: I wanted to be an artist from childhood.

TURNING POINT: Offered an internship at graphics firm senior year of high school.

NEW SITUATION: Learning the challenges of the professional graphics world in the firm.

CHANGE OF PLANS: Graduate from high school, move away, and study art & graphics at college.

COMPLICATIONS: Your art teacher thinks you're too adventurous and experimental at the expense of the conventional technique. You argue with your academic advisor.

MAJOR SETBACK: You run out of college money and also have intractable issues with the art department and bad grades. You leave college.

FINAL PUSH: Move back home, work diligently on your portfolio. Meet another artist at a cafe who inspires you.

CLIMAX: Show a new portfolio to an old internship firm, get hired for your innovative approaches.

MY LIFE SCRIPT

Title:

The Setup:

The Turning Point/Opportunity:

New Situation:

Change of Plans:

Complications:

Major Setback:

Final Push:

Climax:

NOVEL CHARACTER

EXERCISE: Imagine yourself as a character in a novel. Create an original character for a new novel, based on an exaggerated version of yourself.

WHY?: Strong fictional characters come from strong real-life characters. What real person do you spend more time with than anyone else? Yourself. Prolific novelist Holly Lisle, encourages writers to put themselves into their characters, and not just the traits or experiences they'd be proud of, but also ones they'd consider shameful or embarrassing. A great character is usually a complicated, unexpected mess of contradictory qualities. If it's true, it will read as an interesting, believable, and compelling exercise in creative reflection.

IMAGINE YOURSELF AS A CHARACTER IN A NOVEL.

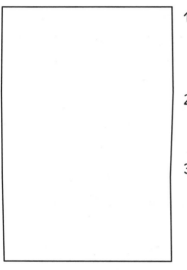

1. How old are they mentally and physically?

2. Did they have a happy childhood? Why/why not?

3. Past/ present relationships? How did they affect Them?

4. What do they care about?

5. What are they obsessed with?

6. Biggest fear?

7. What is the best thing that ever happened to them? The worst?

8. The most embarrassing thing that ever happened to them?

9. Biggest secret?

10. What is the one word you would use to define them?

Please share your #NovelCharacterPS

SCENT MEMORY

EXERCISE: Walk around your home and find some of these common scents. Then, close your eyes and smell them individually for a couple seconds. Keep your eyes closed for 15-30 seconds after you smell and write the memories that flow into your mind. Scent is an excellent vehicle to create visual triggers of events in the past.

"IF YOU'RE LACKING IN CREATIVE IDEAS, GO SMELL SOMETHING"
-Oscar Herman

WHY?: The sense of smell links to our memories, emotions, and life events. Smells can evoke particular memories for your creative brain to reflect on. Everything from citrus, lavender, and mint, to diesel at the gas station and the smell of winter, provides a backdrop to life. This sense memory exercise is a great technique when stuck, and you need to tap into creative reflection for character development.

SCENT MEMORIES

Cinnamon	
Garlic	
Oregano	
Vanilla	
Lemon	
Coffee	
Gasoline	
Leather	
Matches	
Add your own:	

FICTIONAL ROLE MODELS

EXERCISE: Name 3 fictional characters from TV, movies, or books that influenced and inspired you and from whom you borrowed an attitude, outlook, or set of actions. Describe their qualities and actions.

WHY?: Where do our role models and inner voices of strength come from? Sometimes from fiction. That's how influential art can be. Writing in the Guardian newspaper, Richard Lea cites a study showing that almost a fifth of readers claim that fiction filters its way into their daily thinking. Realizing the profound impact that others' creativity has had on you will inspire you to express your own vision, making this is an important aspect of creative reflection.

FICTIONAL CHARACTERS
That Shaped My Reality

CHARACTER:
Qualities:

CHARACTER:
Qualities:

CHARACTER:
Qualities:

MY EULOGY

EXERCISE:

Write your own eulogy, answering questions such as

1. How do I want people to speak of me at my funeral?

2. What should they remember me for?

3. Which kind of person will people think I was when I'm gone.

4. How do you want to be remembered when people talk about you in the future?

WHY?: Mortality can be a great source of inspiration and reflection, even if it's a bit scary to examine. This exercise was made famous by Stephen Covey in his book, "The 7 Habits of Highly Effective People". The goal of examining your death is to help you add more purpose to your everyday activities and the way you live your life. It may help you think twice before reacting to a situation harshly or making a decision before thinking about its possible outcomes. If anything, this exercise in Creative Reflection is about taking stock of your life so far and to encourage you to take risks and make the changes you want as you move into future phases of your life.

MY EULOGY

PROUST QUESTIONNAIRE

EXERCISE: The Proust Questionnaire has its origins in a parlor game popularized (though not devised) by Marcel Proust, the French essayist and novelist. He believed that by answering these questions, an individual reveals his or her true nature. Be like Proust and dare to answer them all!

WHY?: Made popular by Vanity Fair Magazine, The Proust Questionnaire is a self-exploration questionnaire designed to help you uncover your outlook on life and get clarity on how you think. It was answered by Oscar Wilde, Paul Cezanne, David Bowie and many others. This questionnaire distills insights about personality and offers clarity on what one truly values most in life.

THE PROUST
Questionnaire

What is your idea of perfect happiness?

What is your greatest fear?

What is the trait you most deplore in yourself?

What is the trait you most deplore in others?

Which living person do you most admire?

What is your greatest extravagance?

What is your current state of mind?

What do you consider the most overrated virtue?

What or who is the greatest love of your life?

When and where were you happiest?

Which talent would you most like to have?

On what occasion do you lie?

THE PROUST
Questionnaire

What do you most dislike about your appearance?

Which living person do you most despise?

What is the quality you most like in a man?

What is the quality you most like in a woman?

Which words or phrases do you most overuse?

If you could change one thing about yourself, what would it be?

What do you consider your greatest achievement?

If you were to die and come back as a person or a thing, what would it be?

Where would you most like to live?

What is your most treasured possession?

What do you regard as the lowest depth of misery?

What is your favorite occupation?

Please share your #ProustQuestionnairePS

THE PROUST
Questionnaire

What is your most marked characteristic?

What do you most value in your friends?

Who are your favorite writers?

Who is your hero of fiction?

Which historical figure do you most identify with?

Who are your heroes in real life?

What are your favorite names?

What is it that you most dislike?

What is your greatest regret?

How would you like to die?

What is your motto?

LIVE YOUR TRUTH

Please share your #AdultColoringPS

The question isn't who is going to let me; It's who is going to stop me.

A Perceptual illusion is when the brain perceives reality in different ways.

Perceptual illusions provide a keyhole glimpse into creativity and curiosity, as our mind anticipates the future in order to see the present.

Artists often play with perspective and distortion, creating impossible scenarios that bend perception.

What do you see: a rabbit?
or a duck?

The duck-rabbit drawing was first used by American psychologist Joseph Jastrow in 1899 to make the point that perception is not only what you see (and how fast you see it) but could indicate how quickly your brain works - and how creative you are.

His research suggested that the faster you can see the second animal and change your perception of the drawing to switch between the two animals, the more creative you are.

Duck

Rabbit

This image suggests that the horizontal lines are bent; however, the distortion is caused by the background that simulates perspective, and false depth perception is created.

Stare closely at this light bulb for 25 seconds. Then immediately stare at a white wall or sheet of paper.
What do you see?

You should see a glowing bulb.

How many black dots do you count?

Whoa!

Where there is an open mind,
there will always be a frontier.

— **CHARLES KETTERING**,
Inventor, Engineer, and Businessman

Please share your #AdultColoringPS

This is a test to see if your mission in this life is complete, if you are alive, it isn't.

– RICHARD BACH
Illusions: The Adventures of a Reluctant Messiah